The HEART of LOVELINESS

Written by EMILIE BARNES Paintings by DONNY FINLEY

Harvest House Publishers

Eugene, Oregon

I dedicate this book to our daughter, Jenny. I have watched her grow from a baby to a beautiful woman of God. She has had to work through some difficult times in her life, all the while holding on to God's hand. I have hugged and cried with her—and had many laughs as well. She is my daughter but also my best friend. Through my long illness, Jenny has been with me to cry, listen, hold me, feed me, and walk with me through my recovery. She truly has the heart of loveliness. How very proud we are of Jenny—woman, wife, mother, daughter, and child of God. I deeply love you, my princess.
—Hugs, Mom (Grand Mossy)

I would like to dedicate this book to my wife, Janet, and my three daughters, Catie, Leah, and Sarah. Their loveliness inspires me daily.
—Donny

The HEART of LOVELINESS

Text Copyright ©2001 by Harvest House Publishers
Eugene, Oregon 97402

Library of Congress Cataloging-in-Publication Data

Barnes, Emilie.
  The heart of loveliness/Emilie Barnes ; paintings by Donny Finley.
    p. cm.
  ISBN 0-7369-0312-7
  1. Christian women–Religious life. 2. Femininity–Religious aspects–Christianity. I. Title.

  BV4527 .B35874 2001
  248.8'43–dc21

Text for this book has been excerpted from *The Spirit of Loveliness* by Emilie Barnes (Harvest House Publishers, 1992).

Artwork designs are reproduced under license from © Arts Uniq'®, Inc., Cookeville, TN and may not be reproduced without permission. For information regarding art prints featured in this book, please contact:

  Arts Uniq'
  P.O. Box 3085
  Cookeville, TN 38502
  800-223-5020

Design and production by Koechel Peterson and Associates, Minneapolis, Minnesota

Scriptures are from the HOLY BIBLE: NEW INTERNATIONAL VERSION ®. NIV ®. Copyright © 1973, 1978, 1984 by the International Bible Society. Used by permission of Zondervan Publishing House.

Printed in Hong Kong

01 02 03 04 05 06 07 08 09 10 / NG / 10 9 8 7 6 5 4 3 2 1

THE HEART OF LOVELINESS. . .

*Whatever is true, whatever is noble,
whatever is right, whatever is pure,
whatever is lovely, whatever is admirable—
if anything is excellent or praiseworthy—
think about such things.*

—PHILIPPIANS 4:8

THE *Spirit* OF *Femininity*

When I was a little girl, I used to dream of being a "lady." The world of *Little Women*, with its gracious manners and old-fashioned, flowing dresses, fascinated me. Softness and lace, tantalizing fragrance and exquisite texture, a nurturing spirit and a love of beauty—these images of femininity shaped my earliest ideas of loveliness.

Is that kind of femininity a lost value today? I don't believe it. The world has changed, and most of us live in simple skirts or business suits or jeans instead of flowing gowns. But I still believe that somewhere in the heart of most of us is a little girl who longs to be a lady.

I also believe that today's world is hungering to be transformed by the spirit of femininity. What better antidote for an impersonal and violent society than warm, gentle, feminine strength? What better cure for urban sprawl and trashed-out countrysides than a love of beauty and a confidence in one's ability to make things lovely? What better hope for the future than a nurturing mother's heart that is more concerned for the next generation than for its own selfish desires? All these qualities—gentle strength, love of beauty, care and nurturing—are part of the spirit of femininity.

Being a woman created by God is such a privilege—and the gift of our femininity is something we can give both to ourselves and to the people around us. Just one flower, one candle, can warm up a cold, no-nonsense atmosphere with an aura of "I care."

Feminine

Women have always had the ability to transform an environment, to make it comfortable and inviting. I believe we should rejoice in that ability and make the most of it.

This doesn't mean we have to follow a set pattern or adopt a cookie-cutter style. The specific expressions of femininity vary greatly. When I think "feminine," I usually think of soft colors, lace, and flowers. I love ruffled curtains and flower-sprigged wallpaper, delicate bone china and old-fashioned garden prints. And I feel especially beautiful when I'm dressed up in soft and colorful fabrics.

But I know women with vastly different styles who still exude that special quality I call femininity—women who wear their tailored tweeds or their casual cottons (or their gardening "grubbies") with an air of gentleness and sensitivity. Women who fill their sleek modern kitchens or their utilitarian office cubicles with that unmistakable sense of warmth, caring, and responsiveness. Women who combine self-confidence and an indomitable spirit with a gracious humility and a tender teachability. Women who wear the spirit of femininity with the grace and confidence with which they wear their favorite elegant scent.

The spirit of femininity is so many things. To me, it is objects chosen for their beauty as well as their usefulness…and lovingly cared for. It is people accepted and nurtured, loveliness embraced and shared. More important, the spirit of femininity is the spirit of care and compassion. In my mind, the most feminine woman is one with an eye and ear for others, and a heart for God.

Elegant

PERSONAL EXPRESSIONS

At its best, our femininity arises naturally, out of who we are, and finds its natural expression in the way we live our lives and make our homes. But in our hectic, hard-driven society, it's easy to lose track of our gentle, feminine side. The spirit of femininity is something we must nurture in ourselves and in our homes, and celebrate as God's gift to us.

Femininity can be cultivated in many ways. A fragrant oil or a few drops of perfume in the bathwater. A daisy on your desk. A lace scarf or an embroidered hanky in your pocket. A crocheted shawl around your shoulders. Whatever awakens the calm and gentle spirit within you will nurture the spirit of loveliness in your life.

The expression of femininity is a very personal thing, an expression of a woman's unique self. It is closely tied with identity and with style. Many of the most feminine women I know develop a signature or trademark that marks their distinctiveness. One woman always wears hats. Another enhances her distinctive presence with a favorite fragrance. Still another adopts a theme or motif that becomes a part of her identity.

My friend Marilyn Heavilin's theme is roses. All her correspondence is "rosy," whether with a sticker, a rubber stamp, or her own distinctive stationery. Her home, too, is full of roses—on everything from bedspreads to dessert dishes to rose-scented potpourri.

Marita Littauer-Noon, one of my publicists, loves rabbits. When she was little her nickname was "Bunny," and she has carried this trademark into adulthood. Marita and her husband, Chuck, have bunny T-shirts, bunny candle holders, even a ten-year-old live bunny as a pet. Anytime I see anything with a rabbit on it I think of Marita, and at Christmas or on her birthday she always gets a bunny gift. Finding the personalized presents is fun for me and Marita. It's one way of celebrating her unique, feminine personality.

The beautiful woman is disciplined, chaste, discreet, deferring, gracious, controlled, "together." This kind of woman God considers godly, which means she's got his qualities, and she's close to his heart. This is "his kind of woman."

—ANNE ORTLUND

Unique

8

In today's world...
it is still women's business
to make life better, to make
tomorrow better than today.

—Helen Thames Raley

SMALL PLEASURES

The spirit of femininity includes a wholesome sensuality—a rejoicing in the fragrances and textures and sounds of God's world. We honor God and express the spirit of femininity when we get excited about the beauty around us, when we cultivate the senses that God created in us.

What is the first thing you do when you pick a rose? You put it to your nose to enjoy the fragrance. How does it make you feel? Maybe it brings a pleasant memory of that little girl inside you—the time you picked a flower for your mother or grandmother.

Beautiful fragrances can waft the beauty of femininity all around the house. A lavender sachet thrown in your underwear drawer, sewing box, or stocking box—or hung on a hanger in the closet—imparts its delicate fragrance at the most unexpected times. Spray a little cologne on your notepaper, the bathroom throw rug, or even the toilet bowl. Fill your house with pine at Christmas, or boil a little pot of cinnamon and other spices on the stove.

And enjoy your other senses as well. Put on lively music while you do your housework, and take time out to dance before the Lord. Experiment with herbs and spices in your cooking, and don't be afraid to try new dishes. Slipcover a rough-textured sofa with a cool, smooth sheet, and banish your scratchy, uncomfortable sweaters.

There is nothing self-indulgent or worldly about such small pleasures when we approach them with a spirit of gratitude, as God's gifts to help us go about the tasks he has given us. When we feel that the little things in our lives are pleasant and satisfying, it's amazing how the outside stresses and disappointments fade, at least for the moment. We can then regroup, prioritize, and pray—cultivating the spirit of femininity and preparing ourselves to be God's people in the world.

It is the glow within that creates beauty.
People are like stained-glass windows. They sparkle
like crystal in the sun. At night they continue
to sparkle only if there is light from within.

—Bonnie Green

HONORING GOD'S GIFT

*N*urturing the spirit of femininity in our lives begins with caring for ourselves, with celebrating our unique assets of body and spirit.

Look at your body. How unlike a man's it is! The rest of you is different, too—even the structure of your brain. Did you know that women have a higher pain threshold, a keener sense of smell, and better integration between the right and left sides of our brain? I believe we are meant to rejoice in those special feminine qualities that God has gifted us with.

Song of Songs celebrates feminine beauty with wonderful poetry. The woman described there has bouncy, flowing hair (like a flock of goats), sparkling teeth, lips like scarlet ribbons, glowing cheeks, a round and smooth neck, gently swelling breasts, and clothing with the fragrance of Lebanon.

Does that describe me? I hope so. At least, I hope I am taking the trouble to make the best of what God has given me. I may not have time for the twelve months of beauty treatments that transformed a little Jewish girl named Esther into the Queen of Persia. I may never look like a model or a movie star or even my best friend. But I can honor God's gift of my femininity by taking care of the unique me that he has created.

Gifts

That's one reason I try to be faithful to my exercise program. My daily walks not only help me keep my figure under control, but they restore my energy, lift my spirits, and give me a sense of well-being that makes it easier for me to reach out to others.

That's also why I make the effort to eat healthful foods and prepare them for my family. Shining hair, healthy nails, fresh skin, strong teeth, stress control—all relate directly to the food I put in my body.

And that's why I take that little bit of extra time to pluck and color and brush and cream. A fresh haircut, well-shaped nails, soft lips and hands, pink cheeks, curled eyelashes, pressed and mended clothing—these things help me feel more beautiful, and they tell the world that I care enough to cultivate the spirit of femininity in my life.

And that's why I make the effort to surround myself with beauty. When I do, I myself feel more beautiful. I experience the joy of sharing beauty with those closest to me. And I am motivated to reach out to others with gentleness and care.

Surely that beautiful woman in Song of Songs did that. Solomon speaks often of perfume filling the air, of lush wildflowers and morning breezes. Beauty was all around her, from the wildflowers in Sharon to the lily in the mountain valley.

Gentle

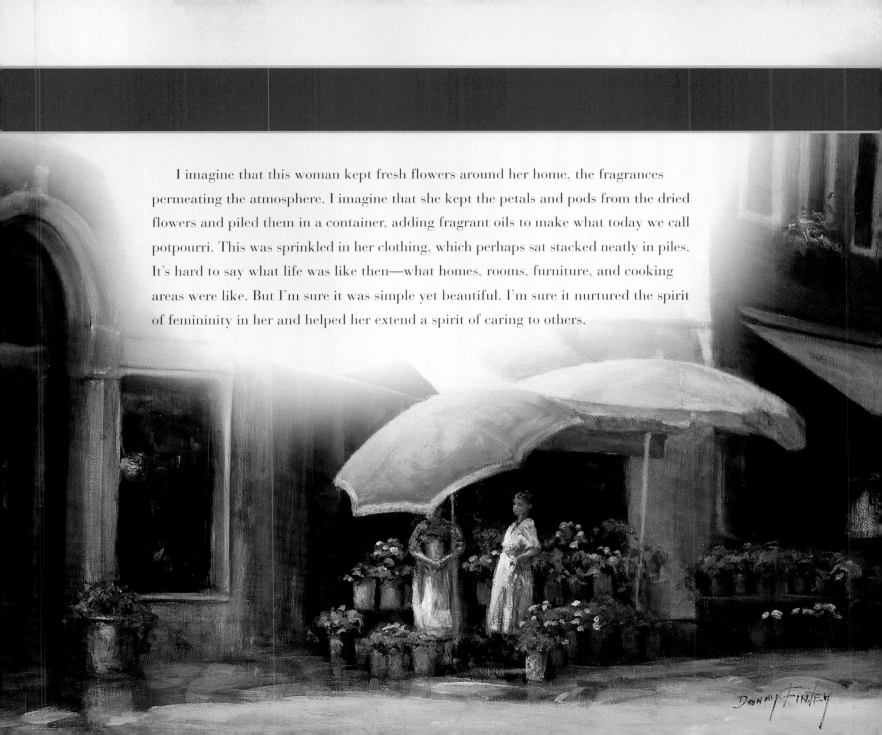

I imagine that this woman kept fresh flowers around her home, the fragrances permeating the atmosphere. I imagine that she kept the petals and pods from the dried flowers and piled them in a container, adding fragrant oils to make what today we call potpourri. This was sprinkled in her clothing, which perhaps sat stacked neatly in piles. It's hard to say what life was like then—what homes, rooms, furniture, and cooking areas were like. But I'm sure it was simple yet beautiful. I'm sure it nurtured the spirit of femininity in her and helped her extend a spirit of caring to others.

FROM THE HEART

As much as I believe in taking care of myself and my environment, I know that if I put all my energy into self-care I have missed the whole point. The true beauty of femininity comes from within. If that beauty is lacking, no exercise program, eating plan, wardrobe update, or beauty treatment can put it there. No interior decorating scheme can give it to me. Ruffles and perfume are no substitute for inner beauty.

The true spirit of femininity comes from the *heart*, and I nurture it when I pay attention to what is truly important in life. That's why I need the message of 1 Peter 3:3-5:

Your beauty should not come from outward adornment, such as braided hair and the wearing of gold jewelry and fine clothes. Instead, it should be that of your inner self, the unfading beauty of a gentle and quiet spirit, which is of great worth in God's sight. For this is the way the holy women of the past who put their hope in God used to make themselves beautiful.

Beauty

NURTURING LOVE

*L*ast Christmas our daughter-in-law, Maria, gave me a small pink satin heart with soft lace around it and a pink satin ribbon to hang it by. The scent is soft and gentle. I keep it hung in my bathroom by my makeup area as a reminder not only of her love and thoughtfulness, but also of God's tender, nurturing love to me.

Do you realize that those are "feminine" words for God? Don't be surprised or put off by that. If we women are made in God's image, it only makes sense that we derive our femininity from him. The Bible's word pictures for God are full of soft, tender "feminine" images. God is not only the powerful father; he also displays a tender, nurturing "motherly" side. We honor God when we rejoice in our femininity and let it transform the world around us.

Femininity is so much more than lace and flowers. A woman with the spirit of femininity is a woman with a teachable heart—a heart that can give and forgive, protect and respect, go from craze to praise. Wrap all that up with a pink satin ribbon (or an earthy, handwoven shawl), and you have the kind of feminine woman that Proverbs says is "worth far more than rubies" (31:10).

The fragrance of that small heart sachet reminds me of the beautiful fragrance of the Lord Jesus himself, and that I am called to be a woman after God's own heart. I

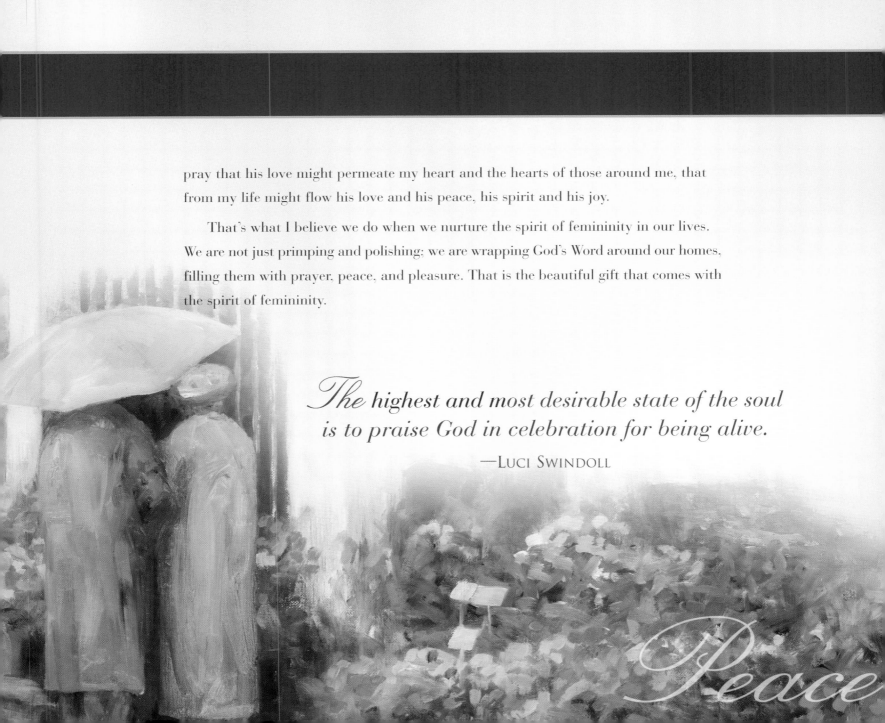

pray that his love might permeate my heart and the hearts of those around me, that from my life might flow his love and his peace, his spirit and his joy.

That's what I believe we do when we nurture the spirit of femininity in our lives. We are not just primping and polishing; we are wrapping God's Word around our homes, filling them with prayer, peace, and pleasure. That is the beautiful gift that comes with the spirit of femininity.

The highest and most desirable state of the soul is to praise God in celebration for being alive.

—Luci Swindoll

Peace

A BEAUTIFUL HERITAGE

*T*he spirit of femininity may be gentle and tender, but it is far from weak. Filling our lives with loveliness takes physical stamina, emotional strength, and spiritual courage. And that's no modern, feminist secret. Beautiful women of all ages have shaped the world with the power of their femininity.

I think of Queen Esther standing in her inner court of the palace, resplendent in her royal robes, risking her life to save her people. Or that admirable (if a bit intimidating) woman in Proverbs 31 running a household and a business while still finding time for volunteer work. Or my own sweet mother, who ran a little dress shop to support us after my father died, and who taught me to love beauty and reach out in love to other people.

Or what about Sarah Edwards, the wife of the famous theologian Jonathan Edwards? In the late 1800's, with no modern conveniences, she ran a household and raised eleven children. She made all the family's clothes, cooked and prepared all the foods, worked the garden, made candles, and stoked the fire. Many guests filled their busy Colonial home. She taught her children to work hard, to respect others, and to show good manners. And she surrounded all her teaching with her love for God and each child.

All of this time, hard work, and love showed up in the children's accomplishments and attitudes. Her children passed on this same love and discipline to their children.

Timothy Dwight, Sarah's grandson and former President of Yale University, said, "All that I am and all I will ever be I owe to my mother."

Strong, beautiful femininity is part of our heritage as women. When we make the effort to cultivate such gentle strength, we not only enrich our own lives and make life a little better for those we encounter; we also pass on the spirit of femininity to the next generation.

In quietness and trust is your strength.
—Isaiah 30:15

LEAVING A LEGACY

Passing on the torch of womanhood is so much more than teaching sewing or flower arranging (and these skills are no prerequisite for femininity). To me, passing on the heritage of femininity is most of all a process of teaching values—caring for ourselves and others, shaping a godly and welcoming atmosphere in our homes and our lives, working hard to affirm life, making the spirit of loveliness a priority.

The time we spend teaching our daughters—biological and spiritual—about the joys and responsibilities of womanhood will provide benefits for generations to come. And we teach best by what we are, not by what we say.

That's why I pray, "Lord, may the love of Christ permeate my heart and life and spread its gentle fragrance into the lives and hearts of those I meet each day. May the gentle but strong spirit of femininity in my life add beauty and meaning to generations to come."

*We cannot make something where
nothing existed—whether it be a poem,
a house, or a painting—without breathing
life into it so that it may itself breathe.*
—ELIZABETH O'CONNOR

A RICH HARVEST

Gardening yields so much in our lives. It lets us participate in God's process of creation. It provides wonderful opportunities for teaching and sharing and giving. But I have found that the spirit of the garden yields a deeper harvest as well.

Over the years, gardening has taught me a lot about who I am as a woman of God. Through many hours of working alone and with others—tilling, planting, mulching, weeding, pruning, repotting—I have learned to "slow down and smell the roses." I have moved closer to a healthy balance between "doing" and "being." That's because the garden forces me to go at God's pace, taking time from a busy schedule of writing, traveling, and speaking to do the simple daily chores that lead to loveliness. It's an eternal rhythm: Sometimes I work, sometimes I wait…then God does the growing and I enjoy the results! I thank God regularly for his gift of the spirit of the garden.

What is bettre than a good womman?
Nothyng.

—GEOFFREY CHAUCER

"Be still and know that I am God," the psalmist urges.

Easier said than done, right?

The complaint I hear from so many women these days is, "I'm just dying for a little peace and quiet—a chance to relax and to think and to pray. And somehow I just can't seem to manage it."

"Stillness" is not a word that many of us even use anymore, let alone experience. Yet women today, perhaps more than at any other time in history, desperately need the spirit of stillness. We are constantly on the move, stretched to our maximum by all the hats we wear, all the balls we juggle, and all the demands our lives bring. In order for the spirit of loveliness to live in us, we must seek out opportunities to rest, plan, regroup, and draw closer to God. And we do that when we deliberately cultivate the spirit of stillness in our homes and in our lives.

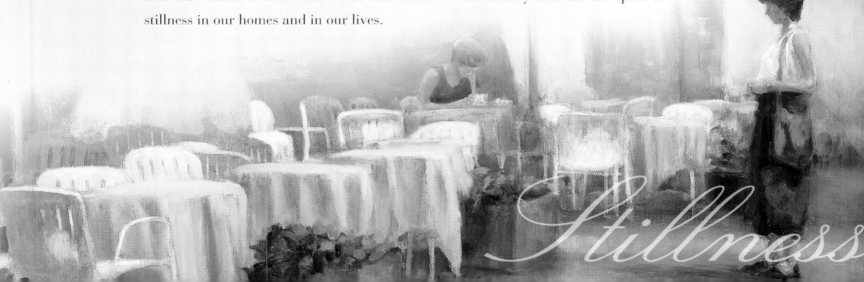

Stillness

MAKING TIME FOR THE INWARD

I've come to realize that all people need to get away from everything and everybody on a regular basis for thought, prayer, and just rest. For me this includes both daily quiet times and more extended periods of relaxation and replenishment. And it includes both times spent with my husband and periods of true solitude, spent with just me and God. These times of stillness offer me the chance to look within and nurture the real me. They keep me from becoming frazzled and depleted by the world around me.

I would say the ideal balance between outward and inward pursuits should be about fifty-fifty. By "outward" I mean working toward goals and deadlines, negotiating needs and privileges, coping with stress, taking care of daily chores, striving toward retirement— getting things done. "Inward" things include tuning in to my spiritual self, talking to God, exploring the sorrows, hopes, and dreams that make up the inner me, and just relaxing in God's eternal presence.

When I was younger, my life was tilted more outward and less inward. As I grow and mature (and perhaps reach another stage of my life), I find I'm leaning more toward the inward. I want my life to be geared more toward heaven. I want to lift my life, my hands, my head, and my body toward God, to spend more time alone with him—talking, listening, and just being. I want to experience the fragrance of his love and let that love permeate my life, to let the calmness of his spirit replenish the empty well of my heart, which gets depleted in the busyness and rush of the everyday demands and pressures.

I want those things for you, too. That's why I urge you: Do whatever is necessary to nurture the spirit of stillness in your life. Don't let the enemy wear you so thin that you lose your balance and perspective. Regular time for stillness is as important and necessary as sleep, exercise, and nutritional food.

Share your life, and find the finest
joy man can know. Do not be stingy with
your heart. Get out of yourself into the
lives of others, and new life will flow into
you—share and share alike.

—JOSEPH FORT NEWTON

Balance

QUIET TIMES

There are some things that can only be accomplished as we meet with the Lord in quiet. It is in our quiet times that we get a handle on so many challenging parts of our lives—unpredictable emotions, worries and apprehensions, needs for approval and reassurance, fears and insecurities, hopes and dreams. It is during these special moments of our lives that we move toward getting things settled with God. Maybe that's why Paul advised the Thessalonians, "Make it your ambition to lead a quiet life…so that your daily life may win the respect of outsiders and so that you will not be dependent on anybody" (1 Thessalonians 4:11,12).

The people who allow themselves time for stillness have made many exciting discoveries—about themselves, about God, and about the kind of life God has in mind. And these people seem to be calm and peaceful and generally have life in perspective. They are people I know in whom the spirit of loveliness seems to flourish. And that's what I want for my life.

Drop thy still dews of quietness
till all our strivings cease; take from our souls
the strain and stress, and let our ordered lives
confess the beauty of Thy peace.

—JOHN GREENLEAF WHITTIER

LISTEN TO THE QUIET

*M*aking space in your schedule for quiet meditation is absolutely vital to infusing your life with the spirit of stillness. But stillness and serenity involve more than a chunk of your schedule. You can also nurture the spirit of stillness by the way you relate to others and by the way you arrange your activities and environment.

Make a point of putting yourself in places that help you slow down, tune out the clamor, and listen to the quiet. Discover the places that foster the stillness in your soul—garden, bathroom, chapel, library, café or coffeehouse, terrace, ocean, lake, mountain, or hammock—and go there regularly.

If you don't know about such a place, ask God to lead you to one. Remember, ours is the God who leads us beside still waters. If we ask, he will take us somewhere that restores our souls.

The outdoors, especially, is a wonderful place to nurture the spirit of stillness. There's nothing like the sun and the breeze on your face or the sound of flowing water to calm your spirit and prepare you for stillness. And you don't have to sit for hours to enjoy the serenity of nature.

In fact, I find that physical exercise actually helps me nurture the spirit of stillness. When I walk along the Gage Canal in Riverside, smelling the orange blossoms as I stride along, I invariably end up thinking of praying and praising. At the same time, something slows inside me. It's almost as if moving my feet helps bring the stillness to my soul.

To me, a godly woman is one who possesses inner peace and tranquility; she doesn't have to prove herself to anyone. She is strong, and yet she doesn't use her strength to control or dominate people; neither does she depend on recognition from others. Hers is an inner contentment and satisfaction based not on accomplishments, position, or authority, but on a deep awareness of God's eternal and personal love for her.

That kind of inner peace, strength, confidence, and tranquility comes from depending on God, obeying him, drawing on his strength and wisdom, learning to be like him. When this happens in our lives, we gradually grow free of anxious competitiveness and aggressiveness. We have no need to prove our worth and value because we *know* how much we are worth in God's sight. And then we are free to reach out in love to others.

I've seen that spirit at work in the lives of so many beautiful Christian women—women of all ages and every walk of life. I think of Lori Martin, who was 25 when I first met her at the Edmonton airport in Alberta, Canada. In the two days we spent together then, I could see the spirit of godliness shining in the life of this young woman. She had a vision for her family and the women of her church to become more Christ-centered, and that vision was contagious. We've been back several times to give our "More Hours in My Day" seminars, and each time Lori and her committee have beautifully organized exciting, creative times together.

Wisdom

I also think of the lovely 92-year-old woman who attended one of my seminars a few years back. This amazing lady sat through all four sessions, scribbling notes the entire time. I remember thinking, "At 92, who even cares?" But this new friend told me she wanted to learn everything she could in life so she could pass on her learning to younger women. Her teachable spirit humbled and blessed me. I only hope that when I am 92 I will be as eager to learn and to grow in God's grace.

Godly values—spiritual awareness, obedience, trust, self-giving love—are so different from the values that seem to run this worldly age. And yet God's strategy for growth and happiness has been around for more than 2000 years. Countless generations of women who have taken it seriously have found that it works. I pray that we might take it seriously as well, growing daily in the spirit of godliness and modeling godliness in our homes and lives.

In recent years we have been obsessed with figuring out what a woman should be allowed to do. God says in his Word a woman can do anything; the point is not what she does but what she is.

—ANNE ORTLUND

Lovely

THE STRENGTH TO CHANGE

Becoming a woman of God begins with making a personal commitment to Jesus Christ. Only he can give us the strength to change. Only he can give us the fresh start that allows the spirit of godliness to grow strong in us.

Second Corinthians 5:17 reminds us, "If anyone is in Christ, he is a new creation. The old has gone, the new has come!" That's what I discovered many years ago when I, a 16-year-old Jewish girl, received Christ into my heart. My life began to change from that moment on, and the years since then have always been an exciting adventure.

It hasn't always been easy. I've had to give up much bitterness, anger, fear, hatred, and resentment. Many times I've had to back up and start over, asking God to take over control of my life and show me his way to live. But as I learned to follow him, God has guided me through times of pain and joy, struggle and growth. And how rewarding it has been to see the spirit of godliness take root and grow in my life! I give thanks and praise for all his goodness to me over the years.

I'm not finished yet—far from it. Growing in godliness is a lifelong process. And although God is the one who makes it possible, he requires my cooperation. If I want the spirit of godliness to shine in my life and in my home, I must be willing to change what God wants me to change and learn what he wants to teach me.

When I was about twenty-six years old, our little family moved to Newport Beach, California. Newport Beach is a beautiful and affluent town—full of sailboats, yachts, and beautiful people. But to me the most beautiful people of all were four older women who took me under their wing and drew me into their Tuesday morning prayer group. For four years I sat with those women as they took God's Word and implemented it in their lives. I remember thinking, "That's the kind of woman I want to be," and in the years that followed I have tried to draw from their example.

Now, thirty-six years later, my four friends in Newport are still doing what they were doing during the years that they taught me—still drawing younger women into their midst, teaching and loving them and modeling what the spirit of godliness is all about. Theirs is a wonderful heritage of godliness that they are passing along to yet another generation. I only hope I am doing the same.

If each moment is sacred—
a time and place
where we encounter God—
life itself is sacred.

—JEAN M. BLOMQUIST

The famous thirty-first chapter of Proverbs is a portrait of the kind of godly woman I want to be. She is hardworking, nurturing, creative. She has a good business sense as well as a finely tuned sense of balance and a delight in her role as wife and mother. Most important, she is a "woman who fears the Lord." And what is her reward for all her efforts? "Her children arise and call her blessed; her husband also, and he praises her" (verse 28).

Such a reward would warm any woman's heart. I know I love it whenever my husband Bob and the children praise me and "call me blessed"! But I am also aware that many of you are godly women who pattern your life after biblical principles but do not receive praise from anyone. Many times you may feel or say, "What's the use? No one appreciates me."

Oh, there have been times in my life when I haven't felt appreciated, but God has taught me through these void periods in my life. I began to realize that God was dealing with me on the level of my motivations and my expectations. He wanted me to do whatever I did to please him, not my husband or my children or anyone else.

When I began to stop expecting people to react in a certain way, I began to act out of proper motivation. I was aiming to please God, not expecting certain behavior from family and friends.

Do you know what began to happen? I stopped expecting praise from my family, but I started getting it! My praise came about when my family was free to be themselves. However, I'm not nearly as hungry for compliments as I once was. I find I am satisfied because I am becoming more used to responding in a godly way to life and its many situations. I have become more aware of who I really am, God's child, and why I am here: to grow closer to him and learn his way of doing things. In the process, I have become far less dependent on other people to feel worthwhile.

In talking to hundreds of women each year, I find that they are vainly trying to find the answers to those same two questions: "Who am I?" and "Why am I here?" If God's answer to these two basic questions of life is not yet engraved on your heart, I pray that you will set out on a journey to be satisfied with your answers. Go to God's Scripture, talk to a godly friend, attend a Bible-teaching church, set aside a part of each day to talk to God in prayer. If you seek sincerely, God will show you the traits of the godly woman he created you to be. Then step out in obedience, depending on Jesus. As you do, the beauty of godliness will begin to shine in your life.

As women of godliness, we have the wonderful opportunity to let our lives sparkle with God's love—if we let him. Almighty God is our guide and shepherd and will give us the spirit of godliness to complete the spirit of loveliness in our lives!

Praise

A PRECIOUS GIFT

The "parlor" was tiny, just an extra room behind the store. But the tablecloth was spotless, the candles were glowing, the flowers were bright, the tea was fragrant. Most of all, the smile was genuine and welcoming whenever my mother invited people to "come on back for a cup of tea."

How often I heard her say those words when I was growing up. And how little I realized the mark they would make on me.

Those were hard years after my father died, when Mama and I shared three rooms behind her little dress shop. Mama waited on the customers, did alterations, and worked on the books until late at night. I kept house—planning and shopping for meals, cooking, cleaning, doing laundry—while going to school and learning the dress business as well.

Sometimes I felt like Cinderella—work, work, work. And the little girl in me longed for a Prince Charming to carry me away to his castle. There I would preside over a grand and immaculate household, waited on hand and foot by attentive servants. I would wear gorgeous dresses and entertain kings and queens who marveled at my beauty and my wisdom and brought me lavish gifts.

But in the meantime, of course, I had work to do. And although I didn't know it, I was already receiving a gift more precious than any dream castle could be. For unlike

Precious

Cinderella, I lived with a loving Mama who understood the true meaning of sharing and of joy—a Mama who brightened people's lives with the spirit of hospitality.

Our customers quickly learned that Mama offered a sympathetic ear as well as elegant clothes and impeccable service. Often they ended up sharing their hurts and problems with her. And then, inevitably, would come the invitation: "Let me make you a cup of tea." She would usher our guests back to our main room, which served as a living room by day and a bedroom by night. Quickly a fresh cloth was slipped on the table, a candle lit, fresh flowers set out if possible, and the teapot heated. If we had them, she would pull out cookies or a loaf of banana bread. There was never anything fancy, but the gift of her caring warmed many a heart on a cold night.

And Mama didn't limit her hospitality to just our guests. On many a rainy day I came home from school to a hot baked potato, fresh from the oven. Even with her heavy workload, Mama would take the time to make this little Cinderella feel like a queen.

My Mama's willingness to open her life to others—to share her home, her food, and her love—was truly a royal gift. She passed it along to me, and I have the privilege of passing it on to others. What a joy to be part of the spirit of hospitality!

MAKING OUR LIVES BEAUTIFUL

*T*here are so many ways to celebrate God's gifts of our lives and our relationships—and of himself! We celebrate when we rejoice in beauty and when we work to make our lives beautiful. We celebrate when we take the time to nurture ourselves and our families. We celebrate through our willingness to share, to love each other, to grow. And we celebrate by opening our lives to the Lord and letting his Spirit fill our lives with loveliness.

I wish for you that spirit of celebration, both little and large, in every corner of your life. I wish you the moments of quiet grace and hours of exuberant rejoicing. In your work and your relaxation, your mealtimes and your bedtimes, your home and wherever you go, may all your living give you cause for celebration.

And again I say, "Amen!"

Welcome is what reflects
God's spirit of love,
joy and happiness.

—EMILIE BARNES